INSPIRATIONAL BASKETBALL SHORT STORIES FOR YOUNG READERS

© **Copyright 2023**
All rights reserved.

This document is geared towards providing exact and reliable information with regards to the topic and issue covered. The publication is sold with the idea that the publisher is not required to render accounting, officially permitted, or otherwise, qualified services. If advice is necessary, legal or professional, a practiced individual in the profession should be ordered.

From a Declaration of Principles which was accepted and approved equally by a Committee of the American Bar Association and a Committee of Publishers and Associations.

In no way is it legal to reproduce, duplicate, or transmit any part of this document in either electronic means or in printed format. Recording of this publication is strictly prohibited and any storage of this document is not allowed unless with written permission from the publisher. All rights reserved.

The information provided herein is stated to be truthful and consistent, in that any liability, in terms of inattention or otherwise, by any usage or abuse of any policies, processes, or directions contained within is the solitary and utter responsibility of the recipient reader. Under no circumstances will any legal responsibility or blame be held against the publisher for any reparation, damages, or monetary loss due to the information herein, either directly or indirectly.

Respective authors own all copyrights not held by the publisher.

The information herein is offered for informational purposes solely, and is universal as so. The presentation of the information is without contract or any type of guarantee assurance.

The trademarks that are used are without any consent, and the publication of the trademark is without permission or backing by the trademark owner. All trademarks and brands within this book are for clarifying purposes only and are the owned by the owners themselves, not affiliated with this document.

Table of Contents

INTRODUCTION: THE MAGIC OF BASKETBALL 5
CHAPTER 1: SARAH'S BUZZER BEATER 7
CHAPTER 2: JAMAL'S SLAM DUNK DREAMS 14
CHAPTER 3: MIA'S TRIPLE-DOUBLE TRIUMPH 20
CHAPTER 4: ETHAN'S FREE THROW REDEMPTION 26
CHAPTER 5: GRACE'S CHAMPIONSHIP JOURNEY 31
CHAPTER 6: ANDRE'S DEFENSIVE DOMINANCE 35
CHAPTER 7: AISHA'S BASKETBALL DREAMS 41
CHAPTER 8: ALEX'S COMEBACK STORY 46
CHAPTER 9: JORDAN'S LEGACY OF GREATNESS 51
CHAPTER 10: EMMA'S THREE-POINT TRIUMPH 55
CHAPTER 11: CHRIS'S COURT VISION 60
CHAPTER 12: BASKETBALL'S HEARTWARMING MOMENTS 65
BONUS 1: POSITIVE AFFIRMATIONS FOR SUCCESS 70
BONUS 2: BASKETBALL KNOWLEDGE QUIZ FOR TEENS 79

INTRODUCTION: THE MAGIC OF BASKETBALL

Hello, aspiring basketball players and supporters! Are you prepared to enter the thrilling world of basketball by stepping onto the court? Twelve incredible stories are in store for you, each brimming with inspiration, aspirations, and the special magic that only basketball can provide.

What lies ahead for you, then? Basketball has the extraordinary ability to influence lives, and this book highlights that power. You will experience a trip through tales that will inspire you to believe in the magic of the game and demonstrate how grit, camaraderie, and passion can produce champions.

But first, let's speak about basketball for a moment before we go into these stories. Consider playing a game with your buddies in which you pass the ball in an effort to get it through a hoop. It's not just about scoring; it's also about teamwork, running, defending, and most importantly, enjoying yourself! Basketball has a special way of bringing people together, whether it is played on school grounds, city courts, or large arenas.

Why are all of us here? the game, which we both adore. Basketball is more than just a sport; it is a universal language. You can find children dribbling and daydreaming in neighborhood parks and backyards. In a similar way to the stories you're about to read, this universal love binds us all together.

So, lace up your shoes, grab a basketball, and let's go on a journey that will encourage you to dream big and perhaps, just perhaps, help you become the next basketball phenomenon!

Thanks again for choosing this book, make sure to leave a short review on Amazon if you enjoy it. I'd really love to hear your thoughts

CHAPTER 1: SARAH'S BUZZER BEATER

Young Sarah had a special affinity with her basketball in the small town of Riverside, where everyone knew one another's names and the streets echoed with kids laughing. With its fading color and scratched surface, it could have appeared worn-out to others, but to Sarah, it was a gem. She joyfully ran home each day after school, threw her bag aside, and began dribbling that ball on the sidewalk in front of her house, losing herself in the rhythmic bounce and echo.

The basketball hoop added an extra unique touch to her games. It wasn't one of those gleaming, retail items. Instead, it was a repurposed old basket that her dad had hung above their garage door. With its slightly bowed rim and torn net, it had seen better days, but Sarah loved it nonetheless. It served as a lesson in maximizing one's resources.

Sarah was clearly a basketball fan. Every time the ball passed through her improvised hoop, it was a tribute to her aspirations. She wasn't just practicing on the driveway; in her mind, she was performing in opulent stadiums to adoring crowds. Every shot, dribble, and game with friends brought her one step nearer to realizing her ambition.

The Dream Begins

Every night when Sarah would close her eyes, the same vivid dream would appear. She would be in a huge stadium similar to the one she had seen on television, with brilliant lights illuminating the court. She could feel the overwhelming thrill of the huge throng as its roar resonated in her ears. The numbers on the scoreboard indicated a tie in the game, and with just a few seconds left, the ball would fall into her hands.

Time would pass more slowly in her dream. The only sound louder than the audience's combined gasp would be her heartbeat. She would take a deep breath and then release the ball in a smooth arc, her focused eyes unwavering and resolute. The stadium would explode in jubilant cheers as the ball swooshed through the goal, signaling the winning shot, celebrating her moment of glory.

But Sarah would grin, clinging to the warmth of her dream, when she awoke in the morning to Riverside's recognizable sounds. The driveway served as her court for the time being, and her supporters were her neighborhood pals. Every game, every match filled with joy, was a treasured moment that brought her one step closer to realizing her ambition.

Joining the Team

Something vivid caught Sarah's eye as she was passing through the crowded school hallway, amidst a sea of chattering people and vibrant lockers. On the school's notice board was a colorful poster showing a basketball shooting toward the basket. Join the Riverside Rockets - Junior Basketball Team, it proclaimed in large letters. Sarah came to a complete stop, her eyes wide as she studied the poster in great detail. She had been waiting for this chance to be a part of something greater and to play on a genuine squad.

She visualized donning the Riverside Rockets uniform, working out with the group, and participating in formal games as her pulse beat fast with excitement and expectation. The concept was exciting. But there was a glimmer of uncertainty tangled up with that excitement. Was she prepared for this? She pondered as she recalled her homemade hoop and fun games with her buddies. What if she tried out but wasn't good enough? she pondered. What if she let her team and, worse yet, herself down?

Sarah exhaled deeply, shaking off the unease. The most important thing, in her opinion, was that she was passionate and determined. She took the decision to give it her all whether she succeeded or failed. Every great journey starts with a single step, so perhaps this poster is the cue she has been looking for.

First Days and Friendly Faces

Sarah held her battered basketball close to her chest as she stood on the sidelines of the basketball court. The Riverside Rockets' first day of practice was a whirlwind of activity, with kids flashing their moves, making passes, and shooting hoops. There was a lot of anticipation and some trepidation in the air. Sarah thought that everyone was dribbling and making shots like they had been playing basketball their entire lives. She was intimidated and just a little bit out of her element, like a tiny fish in a big ocean.

However, Sarah started to see the shift in herself as the initial days turned into weeks. Her footwork and shoots improved with each practice session. Her colleagues' encouraging prodding and the coach's directives began to shape her into a more assured player. It took more than simply natural skill; it required commitment, perseverance, and the will to do better every day. Sarah started to realize that she could succeed on the court if she worked hard enough and had the correct support.

Sarah first met Lily at one of those drills. Lily instantly won Sarah over with her contagious zeal and bright grin. Lily was there with her wise counsel whenever Sarah felt insecure or missed a critical shot. Hey Sarah, always keep in mind that it's not about how you start, but how you finish, she would say, clapping Sarah on the back. Sarah used those words as her mantra, a gentle reminder that each setback just served as a stepping stone toward achievement.

The Big Game

The excitement for the final game increased as autumn leaves gave way to winter frost. The Riverside Rockets were preparing to meet the Maplewood Titans, the league's most formidable club, after putting in a lot of practice time and playing a variety of opponents. Fans of both teams filled the gymnasium, carrying banners and having their faces painted in team colors. There was a mix of excitement and trepidation in the air.

It was obvious from the first whistle that this game would go down in history. On the court, both teams rushed, defending fervently and attacking precisely. The Titans promptly retaliated after each Rockets goal. The gym was filled with a symphony of sounds from the rhythm of bouncing balls, squeaky sneakers, and the cheering crowd. Both teams' players were giving it their all, sweat was running down their brows, and their breathing was hard, yet their spirits never wavered.

The scoreboard showed a draw with just one minute remaining as the time was running out. The gym was at its most intense; you could sense the audience's collective heartbeat and see everyone's eyes glued to the court. Each second seemed to endure longer than the previous one as time seemed to slow down. Then, in a turn that seemed to come from out of her fantasies, Sarah discovered herself in possession of the ball. The outcome of the game was in her hands, and it was her moment, exactly as she had imagined it countless times.

The Buzzer Beater Moment

The players' hammering footsteps and frantic cries echoed in Sarah's racing heart. That one pivotal moment brought together memories of late-night practices in her driveway, endless hours spent with the Riverside Rockets, and counsel from her close friend Lily. It's not about how you start, but how you finish, Lily's voice echoed in the distance. She briefly closed her eyes before taking a long, centering breath and launching the ball toward the basket with all the tenacity she could manage.

The gymnasium fell silent as everyone focused on the ball's path as it gently arched in the air. The buzzer then sounded precisely as the ball trembled through the net, as though in time with the universe. Success! The crowd burst into an exhilarating chorus of applause and cheers; the sound was so powerful that it seemed nearly physical. With an amazing buzzer-beater, Sarah, the girl with the used-up ball and the improvised hoop, had won the game for the Riverside Rockets!

Her teammates, who were overjoyed and smiling with pride, ran over to her and joyfully lifted her to her feet. The atmosphere of happiness was evident. A profound understanding overcame Sarah as she turned to face her coach, friends, and family, all of whom were beaming with pride. Dreams were not simply phantoms of the night; they could sometimes come to life during the day. But they demanded more than just wishful thinking; they required grit, sweat, and steadfast faith. That night, Sarah was more than just a star in her own fantasy world—she was a source of hope for every young person in Riverside who dared to dream large.

Looking Forward

The excitement of winning the title wore off over time, but Sarah's burning love for basketball stayed the same. Even though the season was over, her journey was far from over.

Every drill, every game, and every win or loss had taught her something important. She knew that the way to her dreams would be full of bigger games, tougher opponents, and harder tasks. Sarah wasn't scared, though. She didn't feel tired, though. Every game and practice was not only a skill test, but also a step toward the big dream she had for herself. The win over the Maplewood Titans gave her a new sense of confidence and the belief that she could handle any problem that came her way.

One day, as the sky turned gold and purple from the setting sun, Sarah was back in her garage. The way her old basketball bounced and the shadow of the basket her dad had put up made her feel like she was at home. Here, with nothing but a ball and a dream, her journey began. She dribbled, aimed, and shot with a smile on her face, enjoying the flow of the game she loved. Because Sarah knew in her heart that this part with the Riverside Rockets was just the beginning of an epic story that was still to come.

This story is inspired by the remarkable journey and achievements of Sue Bird, a legendary figure in the world of basketball.

CHAPTER 2: JAMAL'S SLAM DUNK DREAMS

Akron, Ohio, was a city full of life and energy. It had tall buildings that seemed to reach the sky in every direction. Jamal, who was young, lived right in the middle of this urban jungle, where the hum of traffic and the faraway chatter of people walking by were always in the background. Where he played, the tall buildings cast long shadows, making the days seem shorter than they were.

But in the middle of all the gray concrete and constant noise of the city, Jamal found a place that felt like home. There was a small playground tucked away between two old houses. This was where Jamal felt safe. The court's peeling paint, the slightly rusty hoop, and the sounds of kids laughing and playing made him feel better.

Jamal would lose track of time when he had a basketball in his hands. He would dribble the ball around and practice his shots, always imagining himself in a huge stadium full of screaming fans. The worn-out court lines and the writing on the walls didn't matter. In his mind, every shot he took was for a title, every dribble was against a tough opponent, and every dream was to play for the best teams in the country.

<u>A Gifted Pair of Shoes</u>

On a sunny afternoon, Jamal was practicing a new way to dribble the ball while a shadow grew over the court. When he looked up, he saw Terrence, an older boy from the area who was known for how good he was at basketball. Jamal had a secret crush on Terrence because he always saw him playing on the bigger courts with the older kids.

Terrence was holding a pair of worn-out basketball shoes that showed signs of many games. "You know, Jamal," Terrence said with a smile, "these shoes have brought me luck and helped me win many games over the years." He got down on his knees and gave them to the little boy. "I'm too big for them now, but I think you might be the right size for them."

Jamal put his feet in the shoes with a mix of surprise and thanks. They fit him like they were made for him especially. As soon as he stood up, he felt more sure of himself. It wasn't just the shoes; it was also how much Terrence believed in him. As he bounced the ball while wearing his new find, each shot and move seemed more accurate and smooth. Because a player gave him a pair of shoes and believed in him, he felt like he could do better at basketball.

Facing the Bullies

As Jamal's skills on the game got better, he got more and more attention. But not all of the eyes on him were kind. A group of older kids who hung out on the edges of the court started to pay attention. Instead of admiring his ability, they let jealousy cloud their view. They would whisper and laugh to each other, and sometimes Jamal could hear them. "Look at Mr. Superstar over there! He thinks he's the next big thing in basketball," they'd say with a sneer.

Jamal would feel sad when they made fun of him and their voices got louder. When his grandma saw this, she would pull him close and tell him some of her best advice. "Jamal," she would say with a mix of wisdom and kindness in her eyes, "in life, there will always be people who try to bring you down because they can't get to where you are. Remember to let your game do the talking." Jamal found relief in her words, which gave him the strength to face another day.

Jamal was determined to show that he was worth something, so he chose not to fight with the bullies. Instead, he used his anger to work even harder on his practice. Every jump shot, dribbling move, and pass he made was his answer to those who didn't believe in him. And as he kept getting better at the game, the whispers and jokes stopped. Jamal had really let his game speak for itself, and people who had doubted him before were now in awe of him.

The Big Opportunity

Akron started to hear about Jamal's great skills on the basketball court. Now, it wasn't just the kids in the neighborhood who talked about him. Parents, coaches, and even sports reporters in the area were talking about the young player who played with heart and skill. It seemed like every jump, dribble, and slam dunk he did sent ripples far beyond his small neighborhood field.

One bright morning, Jamal was putting on his special basketball shoes when he picked up a package with the

Akron junior team's logo. As he opened it, his heart was racing. It was a call to come! They wanted him to join the team and play junior league games for Akron. Jamal had always wanted a big break like this, a chance to play on bigger stages and show off his skills to even bigger crowds.

Jamal joined the Akron junior team. He wore his favorite shoes and had the spirit of a fighter. Each game added to his rising reputation. Not only was he good at what he did, but he also played with a drive and heart that left people in awe. Match after match, he showed that he wasn't just a local star on the playground, but a champion whose goals went far beyond Akron.

Learning from a Legend

The buzz from a game that had just ended was still in the air. Fans were talking, and players were reminiscing about their best moments. A tall man with an air of dignity made his way through the crowd. As he got closer, people started to talk about how they knew him. It was Coach Carter, who was known as a master of the game and a local basketball icon.

Coach Carter stopped in front of Jamal with a warm smile that went all the way to his eyes. "You've got fire in you, young man," he said, his voice filled with respect. "When I see you out there, it makes me think of myself when I was your age." Jamal listened in awe, hardly able to believe that a figure like that was talking to him. Coach Carter then said, "Why don't I give you some tips? Tell you a little bit about what I've learned over the years?" His offer wasn't just to help Jamal play better; it was also a chance to learn more about how basketball works.

Jamal's training changed when Coach Carter was there to watch. They were no longer just about getting better at shots or moves. The coach stressed the importance of working as a team and made sure Jamal knew that every person on the court was important. He taught Jamal the discipline to train every day and the respect to never forget where he came from, no matter how far he went in basketball. Jamal improved as a player and as a person who truly got the spirit of the game with each lesson.

Slam Dunk Success

As the seasons and years went by, so did the stories about how good Jamal was at basketball. What started as whispers on the streets of Akron became the top story in sports magazines. When he was younger, he used to play basketball on a small neighborhood playground under the open sky. Now, he plays in huge arenas where spotlights shine down on him.

When Jamal's name was on the list, stadiums were always full. Fans, both young and old, wore shirts with his number on them and held their breath every time he got the ball. And when he flew through the air with the ball in his hands to make one of his famous slam dunks, the crowd went crazy. It was a sound that showed admiration, happiness, and pure shock at the magic he made on the floor.

Each game, round of applause, and resounding cheer was a sign of Jamal's journey. From dreaming on the streets of Akron to shining on the national stage, his hard work and desire paid off. He wasn't just playing a game when he jumped, passed, or dunked the ball. He was living his dream and inspiring a lot of other people to do the same.

A Dream Realized

Jamal felt the weight of the moment as he stood in the middle of a large court. The bright lights made the clean wooden floor shine. The crowd's loud cheers when they heard his name brought back a lot of memories. He remembered the small field where it all started, his old basketball with its rough surface, and the slightly worn shoes that Terrence had given him. He remembered how bullies used to laugh at him and try to crush his spirit. He also remembered the wise words and lessons that Coach Carter taught him.

He was the player he was today because of the taunts and hard games he had to deal with. Instead of breaking him, the failures made him stronger and helped him build his success. They made him more determined and taught him what it means to be persistent. With each win, big or small, he was not only getting closer to his dream, but he was also giving hope to a whole generation.

Jamal got ready to do one of his famous slam dunks. He had the ball in his hands and could see the basket. As he took a deep breath and got ready to jump, he felt a deep sense of thanks and understanding. Dreams weren't just things that people made up in their heads; they were real ideas waiting to come true. And as he flew toward the basket, he had one clear thought: the universe makes a way for those who chase their dreams with an unwavering heart and desire to make them come true.

This story is inspired by the incredible journey of LeBron James, who rose from challenges to become one of basketball's greatest legends.

CHAPTER 3: MIA'S TRIPLE-DOUBLE TRIUMPH

In the middle of Atlanta, where buildings touched the sky and streets were always busy, there was a special corner that made people happy. This spot was a basketball court, and Mia was the best player there. Every night, as the sun turned the sky orange and pink, Mia would be on the court with her basketball, making magic happen. The speed of her dribbling, the accuracy of her passes, and the height of her shots all amazed everyone. She did a lot more than just play basketball. Mia danced with the ball.

Mia was more than just a basketball player to the kids in Atlanta. She was a sign of optimism and strength. Boys and girls with dreams in their eyes would crowd around the court and watch Mia play. They would soak up her fire and try to imagine what it would be like to be her. They saw her as an example of what they could do, and Mia always gave them hope by showing them how she did things or giving them lessons when she wasn't practicing.

Mia's life wasn't always a smooth flow, though. Behind the captivating plays and the cheers is a long journey with many obstacles. It wasn't easy to be a girl in a sport where boys usually took the lead. She had to deal with people who didn't believe in her and who thought basketball wasn't a game for girls. But Mia was stronger than that. Every time she had a little bit of doubt, she worked harder, which turned her doubt into drive. She was determined to not only play, but also to do well, showing that ability and passion have no limits.

Breaking the Mold

Mia felt a link to basketball from the first time she touched one. The basketball court was her medium, and every dribble, pass, and shot showed how much she loved the game. But, like many artists, she had people who didn't like her work. There were whispers all around her that were full of doubt and skepticism. Some people would say, "Basketball is for boys," while others would say, "Maybe dancing or something else would be better for you." These people tried to stop her from having big dreams and put a lid on her drive.

But in the middle of all her doubts, her mother was a bright light of hope. When the world says you can't do something, show them you can, Mia's mother would say to her with love and confidence. This advice helped Mia find her way. When people around her said things that made her feel bad, she would think about how much her mother believed in her. It was a trust in her potential, her dreams, and her spirit that was stronger than any criticism.

Mia decided to rise instead of giving in to the doubters. She turned their doubts and skepticism into motivation and power. Every statement, joke, and look of doubt only made her more determined. She doubled the amount of time she spent practicing and stayed on the floor until the last street lights went out. She was on a mission, not just to play, but to break the rules and show the world that passion, skill, and drive don't have anything to do with gender.

A Coach's Faith

Coach Reynolds was one of the many people who would watch Mia play at the neighborhood court. His eyes were always on her. Over the years, he had helped a lot of young players, so he had a good sense for spotting raw ability and potential. But when he saw Mia, he wasn't just impressed by her amazing skills. It was her determination, her stubbornness, and her will to succeed that helped her rise above the whispers of doubt.

Coach Reynolds saw Mia's promise and asked her if she would like to train with him. Mia's game started to change when he gave her advice. She worked on her skills, learned how to play basketball better, and soaked up every bit of information the experienced teacher gave her. They were more than just a player and her teacher; they respected and trusted each other. With every practice, Mia became a force to be reckoned with on the court. She not only scored well, but she also made a name for herself with her passes and rebounds.

As the days turned into weeks and the weeks into months, Mia started doing something that not many people could: getting triple-doubles in games on a regular basis. It wasn't just about how many points Mia scored; she had a well-rounded game that helped her team win in many ways. Once filled with whispers of doubt, the crowds were now filled with cheers and praise. With Coach Reynolds by her side, Mia was breaking down barriers, rewriting the story, and showing how determination and faith can open up a world of possibilities.

A Legend in the Making

Mia's name became more well-known in basketball circles with each passing season. From the crowded courts of Atlanta to the bigger world of college basketball, no one could deny her skills. College scouts started to come to her games with clipboards and talk to each other. They were amazed not only by her skills, but also by her spirit, her determination, and the way she brought a different kind of energy to the game.

Mia's journey wasn't just about the game, though. It wasn't just her impressive numbers or medals that made her stand out; it was also the walls she broke down with every dribble and shoot. When she went out on the court, she didn't just play to win. She played for every girl who had been told she couldn't or shouldn't do something. Mia's story became a sign of hope and a sign of what can be done with just pure willpower and desire.

As Mia's fame grew, she stopped being just a basketball player and became a star. Young girls would come to her games with hopes in their eyes, believing that they, too, could break glass ceilings just like Mia did. Mia's journey taught them a very important lesson: with dedication, hard work, and a passionate heart, there is no dream, mountain, or task that is too big.

The Triumph Continues

Mia felt like it was more than just a game when her sneakers squeaked on the floor. Every dribble, pass, and jump shot had a meaning beyond just getting points. She played for the little girls watching with wide eyes, the young women who practiced hard on empty courts, and anyone who had ever been told they didn't fit. Mia wasn't just playing basketball for fun; she was playing to make a difference, to question the status quo, and to inspire others.

Mia didn't just add points to the scoreboard with each game; she also added pages to the history books. Her consistent triple-doubles weren't just amazing numbers; they also sent a strong message. These weren't just important moments in her life; they were also acts of change that showed the world she was a force to be reckoned with. Each of these things put her name even deeper into the history of great basketball players.

Mia's legacy isn't just about how good she was at basketball. It's also about how she broke down walls outside of the court. She showed the world that ability isn't based on gender and that ceilings are meant to be broken through her hard work, persistence, and unwavering spirit. As she told her story of success, Mia became a symbol of hope. She showed that if you work hard enough, you can not only reach your dreams but also change the way the world sees you.

This story is inspired by the incredible journey of Maya Moore, a testament to passion, dedication, and the power of believing in oneself.

CHAPTER 4: ETHAN'S FREE THROW REDEMPTION

Frankfurt was a small town, but the people there loved basketball a lot. From driveways to the neighborhood park, you could hear the rhythmic bouncing of basketballs at any time. Basketball was more than just a game for the people in the town. It was a way of life, a way to get away, and for some people, like Ethan, it was the beat of their heart.

Ethan stood out on the court because he was tall and lanky, and the setting sun often cast a shadow on his back. The way he moved showed how much he loved the game, and every step, dribble, and pass echoed his hopes of becoming a great basketball player. Every day, he worked on his skills and practiced until it got dark. Everyone could see how set he was. Even though he was smart and worked hard, there was one thing he was bad at: free throws.

Ethan's biggest problem seemed to be the free throw line, which was only 15 feet from the basket. On that line, he wasn't as sure of himself as he usually was because he knew people were watching. It looked like the hoop got smaller and the distance got farther. With each shot Ethan missed, the whispers got louder and Ethan's shoulders got heavier. Even though he practiced a lot and loved the game, he couldn't figure out why he failed at something that seemed so easy.

The Taunting Tease

It wasn't a secret that Ethan had trouble making free throws, especially in the close-knit community of Frankfurt. Word got around, and soon everyone in the playground called Ethan "Ethan the Miss." Every time he walked by, a group of voices would sound like a missed shot and then a group of voices would laugh. "Watch out!" they'd say with a smile. "Ethan's going to show us how to miss in style!"

Even though the jokes hurt, Ethan found comfort in the stories of great basketball players, especially his hero Dirk Nowitzki. He had read that Dirk had to deal with a lot of problems early in his career, like getting used to a new country and fighting against how people thought of European players. Dirk's path was full of problems, but he conquered each one with hard work and a strong desire to get better. Ethan got strength from Dirk's story, which showed him that even the best players had hard times.

Ethan didn't want the jokes to define him, so he turned his anger into drive. He didn't let the taunts get to him, though. Instead, he spent extra time at the court practicing free throws as the sun went down. Every miss was a chance to learn, and every book was a lesson to work harder. He was determined to do his job, which was to make his weakest link his strongest.

A Helping Hand

On a sunny afternoon, Ethan went to the local court to play basketball. The sun made long shadows on the court as he tried over and over to make free throws. Every time he missed, he sighed, and each success, even if it was rare, was a small win. He was so focused on practicing that he didn't even notice when Mr. Jensen slowly walked toward the court. He was known all over Frankfurt as a former basketball coach with a lot of experience. He had watched a lot of young players grow up while he was their coach.

"Hey there, Ethan," Mr. Jensen said with a friendly smile. He leaned against the fence and watched Ethan with his eyes. "I've seen you working hard out here day after day. "How about if I give you a few tips?" he asked. At first, Ethan was shocked, but then he felt a surge of hope. Here was a person who could really help him get through his problem.

Ethan started to see where he was going wrong when Mr. Jensen was watching him. The old coach went over the small details, like how important it is to have a proper stance, how to keep your grip steady, and how to keep your eyes on the target. Ethan learned something new from each tip. It wasn't just about throwing the ball; it was a beautiful mix of science and art. Every time Ethan took a practice shot, he felt more confident, and under Mr. Jensen's direction, he slowly changed.

The Big Game and Big Redemption

Ethan had worked hard for months and spent a lot of time on the court to get to this point. The game for first place. The gym was full, and there was a lot of stress and excitement in the air. As time ran out, the scores stayed the same, and Ethan's young shoulders started to feel the weight of the game. When the whistle blew, he stood at the free throw line, where he had been so many times before. His mind was full of memories of missed shots and boos. But among those scary images, he also remembered Mr. Jensen's wise words and Dirk Nowitzki's strong will.

Ethan paused, closed his eyes, and took a deep breath. The crowd's talk turned into a soft hum. He remembered every lesson and hint—the stance, the grip, and the way to look. As he threw the ball, it seemed like time slowed down. It flew through the air with ease, and the lights above it showed where it went. Then, "swish!" As the ball went through the net, it moved around. As Ethan got ready for his next shot, everyone in the room held their breath. And again, he scored with the same calm accuracy. Everyone cheered in the gym, but for Ethan, it was about more than just points on the board.

That night, Ethan was not only the hero of the game, but he also became a sign of strength. On that court, the boy who had once been laughed at was now known as "Ethan the Clutch." His journey showed that anyone could solve any problem as long as they worked hard, got help, and believed in themselves. Even though the championship trophy was a visible sign of his team's success, Ethan's real win was beating his own fears and doubts.

This story is inspired by the perseverance and determination of the legendary basketball player, Dirk Nowitzki.

CHAPTER 5: GRACE'S CHAMPIONSHIP JOURNEY

In the beautiful coastal city of Saint Harbor, the rhythmic bounce of a basketball and the faraway cheers of onlookers were as common as the gentle crash of ocean waves against the shore. Basketball wasn't just a hobby for the community; it was a big part of what made them who they were. The grassy beach courts, surrounded by tall palm trees, were often the center of activity and saw a lot of intense games from dawn to dusk.

Grace stood out among the other players, and it wasn't just because she was tall and commanded attention. Even though she was in a tough race, she kept a cool head. She reminded me of a quiet morning in the bay. But what really made her stand out was not just her amazing skill or her natural understanding of how the game works. It was her uncanny ability to bring together different players into a team that worked well together. She could quickly see each player's unique skills and, like a seasoned conductor, combine them into a beautiful, well-coordinated symphony on the basketball court.

Many people in Saint Harbor played basketball, but Grace lived it. She put in a lot of time to improve her skills, whether it was a solo practice session at dawn or a tough match in the middle of the day when the sun was very hot. But most of all, it was her natural ability to make people get along and work as a team that made her the heart and soul of the basketball scene in the neighborhood.

Stepping Up as a Leader

As Grace moved into high school, rumors started to spread around Saint Harbor about how good she was on the court. People didn't just talk about how good she was; they also talked about how she could get everyone to work toward the same goal. When the time came, it wasn't a big surprise that her high school team picked her to be the captain. But for Grace, wearing the captain's armband was more than just a sign of authority. It was a promise to lead her team with the utmost honesty.

Grace's way of leading was a lot like that of the great basketball player Tim Duncan. She wasn't the type to take over a chat with loud statements or pep talks. Instead, she thought that the best way to lead was to show others how to do it. She gave her all in every practice, drill, and game, not for personal praise but for the good of her team. Every move she made showed how much she cared about the game and her friends. Off the court, she would often help her friends improve their skills or plan the next play, making sure that everyone felt important and heard.

One of Grace's best sayings became the team's motto: "A star can win a game, but a team can win a championship." It showed how much she valued the group over the person. As games turned into seasons, this way of thinking would shape the team's culture, reminding each player that even though each player's best moments were celebrated, it was their strength and unity as a whole that would lead them to success.

The Challenge Ahead

On the way to the title, there were a lot of problems. When Grace and her team played some of the best teams in the league, they were often pushed to their limits. There were games where they were behind by a lot, and it looked like their hopes of winning a title were fading. Key players kept getting hurt, which took them out of the game and made a tough situation even worse. People in the changing room started to wonder if they had the strength to make it through the trip.

But it was when things were hard that Grace really showed she was a leader. She tried to be as strong and cool as Tim Duncan, who she looked up to, because the team's hopes rested on her shoulders. In team meetings or pep talks in the locker room, she didn't talk about depression or division. She would say, "Remember who we are," a lot. "We're more than just a group of individual players; we're a family." Grace gave their campaign new life by using the strengths of each team member and the ties they'd made over the course of the season. They played every game like it was their last, worked out more, and made better plans.

The day of the event finally came. People were talking, and the stakes were bigger than ever. Both teams fought hard, and several times the lead changed hands. As time ran out,

Grace's team stood out because of how hard they worked and how well they worked together. They played for each other and trusted each other, and when the final buzzer went off, they were the ones on top. As they lifted the title trophy high to the sound of roaring cheers, the city of Saint Harbor saw more than just a basketball win. It showed how strong unity, persistence, and steady, quiet leadership can be over time.

Inspired by the quiet leadership and team-centric play of the legendary basketball player, Tim Duncan.

CHAPTER 6: ANDRE'S DEFENSIVE DOMINANCE

In the middle of Detroit, where engines roared in a steady beat and children laughed, one old basketball court stood strong. This court, which was between brick buildings and busy streets, looked like it had been used for many years. Its painted lines were a pale ghost of what they used to be, and the metal hoop, even though it was rusty, still stood proudly, a witness to countless shots taken over the years. But for Andre when he was young, this wasn't just any court; it was holy ground.

Many of the kids who played there wanted to wow the crowd with amazing dribbles, slam dunks, and game-winning shots. Most people wanted to score goals and get the attention that came with it. Not Andre, though. Even though he knew how to score, he was more interested in something else. He loved defense because it was the unsung star of the game.

He got a special thrill out of blocking an opponent's shot or grabbing the ball in midair. It was about waiting, being patient, and knowing the right time to step in. Andre found his real calling on that old Detroit court through his quiet, steady love of defense.

The Wall of Detroit

Andre stood out on that old court in Detroit not because he was tall, but because he was so determined and had so much heart. Andre was there every time an opponent tried to score, blocking their way, stopping their shots, and stealing their chances. His unshakable attitude on the court reminded me of a fortress wall, which doesn't move or change. It didn't take long for the neighborhood kids and people watching to call him "The Wall of Detroit."

When people asked Andre how much he loved defense, his eyes would light up. "Imagine being a superhero," he'd say, grinning widely. "They swoop down from the sky or run across the city, and they always save the day just in time. When I defend, I feel like that. I'm keeping an eye on our hoop to make sure nothing bad happens to it. "Same way those superheroes protect their cities!"

Ben Wallace, a basketball "giant" known not only for his height but also for his legendary defense skills, gave him the drive to work hard. Andre had seen Wallace's games over and over again, paying close attention to every move, choice, and jump. He wanted to be like his hero, a tall, proud defender who stood out in the fast-paced world of basketball.

Challenges and Teasing

Defense, especially the kind of defense that Andre was crazy about, didn't always get the attention it earned in Detroit, where there were lots of loud cheers and fast plays. In a world where making goals and dribbling tricks were praised, Andre's decision to focus mostly on defense made some people look at him funny. Some of the bigger kids on the court just couldn't help but make fun of him. "Hey, Wall," they'd say with sarcasm in their words, "when are you going to shoot?" Or will you just stay behind your walls?"

But these jokes didn't stop Andre much. Whenever their words hurt, he would remember the stories he had read about his hero, Ben Wallace. Even when he was at his best, Wallace had enemies and people who didn't believe in him. But he didn't let those voices make him who he was. Instead, he used them as fuel and turned every criticism into a step toward greatness.

Andre had a similar way of thinking, so he worked harder than ever to learn the art of defense. When the court lights made long shadows late at night, Andre would still be playing. He watched videos of great basketball players and took careful notes on how they defended, where their feet were, and how fast their reactions were. He worked on jumping higher, responding faster, and figuring out how his opponent would move. Every joke and question thrown his way only made him more determined to become the best defender Detroit had ever seen.

The Big Tournament

On the day of the local basketball event, which everyone was looking forward to, the sun was shining brightly. Teams from all over the country came together to show off their skills. Banners flew, whistles chirped, and sneakers squeaked. One of them was Andre's team, the Detroit Defenders, which was a good name for them. People in the crowd could feel the excitement. The Defenders were about to face their toughest opponent yet: the Highflyers, who were known for their flashy offense and quick goals.

As soon as the first whistle blew, the Highflyers showed how good they were. They dribbled and shot with style and seemed to be able to get around the Defenders with ease. The scoreboard started to tilt in a scary way in favor of the Highflyers. But just when things seemed to be going badly, Andre found his groove. He set himself up in a way that stopped the Highflyers at every turn. His eyes were as sharp as a hawk's. Every time he jumped, he blocked a shot that looked like it was going in, and every time he ran, he stopped a pass or stole the ball from the Highflyers.

As the game went on, the crowd's chants of "Fly, Highflyers, Fly!" were slowly drowned out by a new cry. "Go Wall! Go Wall!" they yelled as Andre's great defensive play changed the way the game was going. Not only did he stop the Highflyers, but he also gave his friends hope, boosted their morale, and turned the game around. Andre didn't just play defense; he showed everyone what the Detroit Defenders are all about.

Victory Through Defense

As the final seconds passed, the stadium was filled with a lot of energy. Everyone was on edge, from the players on the bench to the people in the back rows. The score was even, and the Highflyers had control. After a quick, well-planned play, one of their best players got the ball and ran towards the basket. It looked like he would make that last shot that would win. Andre, however, had other ideas. He made his move with the drive that comes from training for a long time and a strong desire to defend himself. He timed his jump correctly and flew up with his hand outstretched just in time to deflect the ball. When the buzzer went off, everyone held their breath. It was time to leave.

As soon as the extra minutes started, there was a lot going on all over the court. Players on both teams moved with purpose and meaning, even though they were tired and on edge. But in the middle of all this chaos, the Detroit Defenders had a secret weapon: Andre, the "Wall of Detroit." Because of how good he was at defense, the Highflyers kept making mistakes, which gave the Defenders more chances to score. Slowly but surely, the Defenders started to pull ahead. They did this by turning Andre's stops into important points.

When the closing whistle blew, the scoreboard told a story that many people hadn't expected. With Andre's unstoppable defense, the Detroit Defenders had won the title. As Andre's teammates put him on their shoulders, the message was clear: sometimes a good defense is the best way to attack. The Defenders had not only won a game, but also earned respect and love by showing how hard work and teamwork can pay off.

A Hero's Recognition

As the sound of the final whistle faded, a loud cheer came from the court. Players, coaches, and fans crowded around

Andre because he was the star of the moment. With admiration in their eyes, his friends put him on their shoulders and carried him around as if he had just won them the world. The rhythmic cry of "Defense! Defense!" filled the air. It was a tribute to Andre's great skills, which had turned the game around. The whole scene was a show of pure joy and admiration, and it was all about a young boy who had worked so hard at his skill.

During the party, a few people from the other team came up. Players from the Highflyers were there, with their heads held high even though they had lost. They reached out to him, not out of anger but out of respect for how well he played. Their compliments and warm handshakes showed great sportsmanship by recognizing ability and effort, no matter what team they were on. This was a beautiful lesson that basketball isn't just about winning. It's also about respecting and appreciating each other, the game, and the players.

That day, Andre's achievement went down in history. But more than the praise and cheers, he taught everyone there a very important lesson: the power of defense in basketball is undeniable. Even though dunks and three-pointers get most of the attention, it's really the stops, steals, and tight defensive plays that can make or break a game. Andre was the perfect example of a dominant defense because he was like his hero, Ben Wallace. And as the sun went down on that memorable day, it was clear that Andre's legacy as a defensive titan had only just started.

This story of Andre's unwavering commitment to defense is inspired by the legendary basketball player, Ben Wallace, whose prowess on the court redefined the importance of defense in the game.

CHAPTER 7: AISHA'S BASKETBALL DREAMS

Every morning, the birds in the peaceful town of Liberty would chirp in tune with the soft colors of the golden sunrise. Usually quiet and calm, the streets would slowly start to come to life. But the rhythmic bounce of a basketball could be heard from the neighborhood court before the town was fully awake. It was Aisha; the early light made her outline dance.

She would get there with her shoes tied tight, and each step would show how determined she was. Her daily routine was to do practice, work on her shots, and get better at dribbling. The sweat on her forehead and the fire in her eyes showed that she had dreams that were bigger than the town.

Every time she took a shot, she saw herself not only on the neighborhood court, but also in big arenas full of cheering fans. She would picture herself playing with or against legends, especially Sheryl Swoopes, who was her favorite player of all time. With love and the desire to make this dream come true, this dream became clearer every day.

Doubts and Determination

In the small town of Liberty, where everyone knew each other, Aisha's dreams came up in many talks. Even though many people liked how determined she was, she often heard whispers of doubt. "Basketball isn't really a game for girls," some people would tell her, giving her suspicious looks. Others would laugh and say, "You think you can play in the big leagues?"

But Aisha had a secret weapon: the stories that Sheryl Swoopes told that gave her hope. She had grown up hearing about how Sheryl, a shining star in women's basketball, had gone against all chances and doubters. Sheryl did more than just play the game; she also changed the story. Every time Aisha heard someone doubt or make fun of Swoopes, she would think of his story to remind herself that greatness often comes from hard times.

Every time the ball went back and forth, Aisha got more determined. She would whisper, "Watch me," as a promise to herself and the world. As the sun went down, her silhouette against the orange sky showed how strong her will was. She took power from heroes of the past and made a way for the future.

A Coach's Belief

The basketball court was always loud with the sounds of bouncing balls, cheering crowds, and the odd referee's whistle. One player, Aisha, stood out not only because she was good, but also because she had fire in her eyes. She played with so much heart and drive that no one could ignore her. It didn't take long for someone very important to notice how hard she worked.

Coach Martinez was a well-known and admired figure in the basketball world. Over the years, he had helped many young players on their way to becoming stars. One sunny afternoon, as Aisha worked hard to get better at shooting, he came up to her with a curious look on his face. "You know," he said as he watched her make a beautiful layup, "you remind me of a young Sheryl Swoopes." He didn't just say nice things about her; he also told her she had a lot of promise.

Coach Martinez made an offer because he saw a chance to make yet another star. "How would you like to have some special training sessions?" Aisha agreed quickly and with a sparkle in her eyes. Under his careful watch, Aisha's natural ability got better. They got better at every move, pass, and jump shot. With Coach Martinez's advice and Aisha's hard work, she changed over time and became a force to be reckoned with on the basketball court.

The Big Tournament and a Star's Rise

Every year, when the yearly Liberty Basketball Tournament got closer, the town of Liberty was full of excitement. It was more than just a sports game; it was a gathering that honored people with skill and drive. This year, there was even more excitement in the air. Everyone was looking at one player, Aisha, who was going to be the leader of her team, the Liberty Larks.

As the game went on, everyone talked about how good Aisha was on the court. Every game she played was a combination of skill, speed, and being a leader. She dribbled, passed, and shot her way into the hearts of the crowd. For the older people there, she reminded them of a young Sheryl Swoopes. Under Aisha's leadership, the Larks seemed unbeatable as they glided through the rounds, leaving behind a trail of impressed fans and defeated opponents.

The day of the finals started out clear and bright, and there was a lot of stress in the air. The Liberty Larks were going up against their biggest foes, the Thunderhawks. The Thunderhawks are known for playing hard and making smart moves. From the beginning to the end, it was a nail-biter. Every time the Larks made a goal, the Thunderhawks scored one of their own. But Aisha, who had the heart of a real winner, got her team back together. The time ran out, and with just a few seconds left, Aisha got the ball. She moved around and dodged, and then she shot with the skill of a pro. Just as the buzzer went off, the ball went through the net. The Liberty Larks won, and Aisha's star got bigger and brighter.

A Legacy Begins

Everyone in Liberty was happy and waving flags in the town square. People cheered and clapped rhythmically in the streets to celebrate a win that was much more than just a game. At the center of all this joy was Aisha, whose excellent play had not only helped the Liberty Larks win, but also given many young people hope for their own dreams.

Every basket Aisha made and every move she mastered on the court sent a strong message. She was the perfect example of grit, showing that with desire and hard work, you can break through any barrier. Young girls watched her with stars in their eyes. They saw not only a basketball player, but also a sign that their goals, no matter what gender they were, were valid and possible.

But more than the awards and praise, Aisha's real impact was the hope she gave to others. People would tell stories about her matches, the difficulties she faced, and how she never gave up. These stories would inspire people for years to come. She wasn't just playing a game. With every dribble and shot, she was making a way, inspired by her hero, Sheryl Swoopes, who never gave up. In Liberty, a legend was born, and the story of Aisha's basketball hopes would always show how important it is to follow your dreams no matter what.

This story is inspired by the tenacity and trailblazing journey of the real-life basketball legend, Sheryl Swoopes.

CHAPTER 8: ALEX'S COMEBACK STORY

The rhythmic sound of basketballs hitting the ground became a recognizable anthem that echoed through the streets and alleys that connected them. As the sun started to go down, it would throw long shadows and turn the courts a golden color. Kids would rush to these urban playgrounds, laughing and shouting along with the sounds of the game.

Even though there were a lot of new players, one person easily stood out. Alex was a natural because of how tall he was and how gracefully he moved. Every smooth move and well-placed shot showed how much he loved and cared about the game. Evening after evening, as the city lights came on, he would stay and work on his jump shots, improve his footwork, and try to run faster and jump higher.

He often had that faraway look in his eyes, which showed that he dreamed of packed stadiums, roaring crowds, and a brightly lit court where he would shine. He wanted to be as good as his basketball hero, Paul George, who told him stories about how hard he worked and how skilled he was.

The Unexpected Setback

Every player knows that playing sports comes with risks, but that doesn't make it easier when something bad happens.

Alex's life changed in a moment on a cool Riverside evening in front of a large crowd. As he rushed toward the basket with his eyes on it and ready to slam dunk, the environment was electric. Everyone in the crowd could feel the excitement as they waited for the familiar swoosh of the net.

But when Alex launched himself into the air, the happiness didn't last long. When they landed, a mistake sent waves of fear through the crowd. With a gasp and a twist, Alex fell to the ground, his face wracked with pain. The court, which had always been a place of happiness and hope for him, became a place of pain all of a sudden. The first diagnosis was bad news for everyone who heard it: Alex had a serious injury that would keep him out of action for what seemed like months and months.

The Long Road to Recovery

Even though time can heal, it can also move slowly and be annoying. Alex's laughter and the sound of his basketball once filled the Riverside courts, but now they seemed like they were on the other side of the world. In his thoughts, the memories of quick moves, quick passes, and cheering crowds kept playing like an old film reel. But as each new day came, a wave of hope came over him. Alex found strength in the stories of his hero, Paul George, who had also been through a rough time in his life. He learned from these stories that losses were just the beginning of comebacks.

Around him, a group of people who always stood by him grew stronger. His family, who had always been there for him, stood by him and gave him strength during the hard times. His friends came to see him and told him stories from the court, making sure he never felt alone. Then there was Dr. Riley, the osteopath who never gave up. His knowledge and support were very helpful. Every lesson was a mix of hard work, sweat, and sheer will. The road was long, and it was full of hard workouts and a lot of therapy. But Alex was sure that he would play again. His heart was full of dreams, and his spirit wouldn't let him give up.

The Triumphant Return

Alex could feel the mood as he walked onto the court, which used to be like his second home. Not only was he excited, but the memories that came back to him also made his heart beat fast. The court had seen him at his best and at his worst, and now it was waiting for him to come back. As he put on his shoes, doubts tried to creep in, but the crowd and his friends quickly drowned them out.

The ball's familiar weight made me feel better. With the first dribble, the rhythm came back. It was as if the beats of the ball on the floor matched his heartbeat. As the game went on, it became clear that Alex wasn't just playing a normal game. Instead, he was making a statement about how hard times hadn't stopped him. Every pass, jump, and shot he made was full of feeling and showed his journey from pain to victory.

By the end of the game, everyone was amazed by how well he had done. But for Alex, it wasn't just a game; it was his song of salvation. It showed that if you are strong, determined, and have a little hope, you can get through anything and get back to your dreams.

A New Legend is Born

People in Riverside talked about Alex's amazing comeback on the streets and in the alleys. People of all ages could relate to his story because it was about more than just a basketball player regaining his spot on the court. It was a story that spoke to every hope who had ever had something go wrong. Cafes, schoolyards, and parks were full of people talking about Alex's successful return. Each story was more exciting than the last.

Alex wasn't just a local hero for a while, but soon he became a sign of never giving up and never giving in. Parents would tell their kids about his story and tell them to never give up when things get hard. Teachers used Alex's story to show how tough and determined people can be. Young players, both pros and beginners, would wear rings with his name on them. Whenever they were feeling down, they would think of his story and feel better.

But what really made Alex stand out was how humble he was about his new position. Even though he was a source of hope for a lot of people, he always said that his story wasn't special. He talked a lot about his hero, Paul George, and how his story of coming back from bad times gave him hope. By doing this, Alex's story became more than just one person's triumph over adversity. It became a symbol of the strength of the human spirit as a whole, passed down from one legend to the next and inspiring people to follow their goals no matter what.

This story is inspired by the resilience and determination of the real-life basketball player, Paul George.

CHAPTER 9: JORDAN'S LEGACY OF GREATNESS

In the pretty town of Windyville, a light breeze always blew through the streets lined with trees, bringing with it the sounds of cheers from basketball courts all over town. Basketballs seemed to be bouncing in every direction, but one court in particular caught the attention of many people. Every day, you could find young Jordan here working on his game.

Jordan's dreams took off with every determined throw and every brave jump. He pictured himself taking the shot that would win the title in front of roaring crowds in huge arenas. His boots, which he had saved up for, looked like the ones the greats wore. But what most people found cute about him was the way he would aim for the basket with his tongue just a little bit out. It wasn't just a strange habit; it was Jordan's way of paying respect to the basketball player he admired most, the great Michael Jordan.

Chasing the Hoop

Jordan would hurry to finish his homework every night as the sun set and cast a nice golden glow over Windyville. With every stroke of his pen, he was getting more and more excited to go to the playground, which he loved. Even though the air was filled with the sounds of jump ropes and soccer games, Jordan's corner of the field was still only for basketball.

His friends would often make fun of him because they were always up for something new and active. "Jordan, come on! How about a game of soccer?" They would call out with smiles on their faces. Without skipping a beat, Jordan would laugh heartily and say, "Have you ever seen Michael Jordan glide through the air? So, that's why!" As if on cue, he would grab the ball, run quickly, and shoot one of his trademark jump shots. The ball would fly through the net, making people around the playground look on in awe. At that time, people who were watching thought that young Jordan wasn't just trying to be like his hero; they thought he was MJ himself.

Overcoming Hurdles

Windyville's basketball court had seen its fair share of wins and loses, and Jordan, with his unwavering passion, was at the center of many of them. But the way to becoming a great player wasn't smooth; it was full of obstacles. Some days, the ball just wouldn't behave and wouldn't go through the net. Even though he tried hard, there were times when he missed that all-important shot, and his heart was heavy with sadness.

But even during these hard times, Jordan found comfort and motivation in stories about Michael Jordan, the basketball player who was his hero. He would often tell stories about how even Michael Jackson had his own problems. The story of Michael getting cut from his high school basketball team, which could have broken many people, really got to the young boy. But instead, it made Michael want to be the best at his sport ever. Jordan would wipe away his sweat and sometimes his tears and then go back out on the floor. He worked harder, stayed on the court until the sun went down, and kept a strong belief in what he was capable of. Every time he fell, Jordan was motivated to get back up, just like his hero.

The Championship Game

The sun was shining brightly over Windyville, but the excitement in the air was even brighter. As the people of the town gathered, you could feel their energy. The kids put on their team outfits and talked about how to win. It was the day of the Windyville Basketball Tournament, an event that brought people together who loved basketball. The courts looked brand new, and the hoops seemed to be waiting for something to happen.

Everyone had been looking forward to this match. Jordan's team, the Windyville Wizards, was playing against their biggest foes, a team that had won many games but had never faced a player with Jordan's drive. It was clear from the start that this wasn't just any game. Everyone was on the edge of their seats for every pass, move, and shot. Both teams were very skilled, and they tied each other point for point. In the last few minutes, the stress reached its peak. Both teams had the same number of points, and time was running out. With only a few seconds left, the ball got to Jordan. Time seemed to slow down as he got in place and thought about every practice, lesson, and idea he got from Michael Jordan. He took his shot by taking a big breath and sticking out his tongue in his usual way. The ball went through the net with a beautiful curve. The crowd went crazy with joy. The Windyville Wizards had won the game because Jordan was so skilled and never gave up.

A Star in the Making

Everyone in Windyville was talking about the recent basketball event, and Jordan was at the center of every story. The once-familiar basketball court was now constantly filled with people who wanted to see the young star play. The story of how he won the game with a shot that was inspired by the great Michael Jordan was told over and over again, each time with more respect and awe.

As the days turned into weeks, Jordan went from being just another kid who wanted to play basketball to being a hero in his town. Parents would talk about how hard he worked, how much he practiced, and how strong he was in the evenings. They showed him to their kids and said, "See? If you work hard and have passion, you can do anything!"

The basketball court became a place where people got together not just to play games but also to get ideas. Little kids would copy Jordan's moves with stars in their eyes, thinking that one day they too could leave a great legacy. And even though he was getting a lot of attention, Jordan kept practicing. He was humble about his success, but he was always motivated, showing everyone the power of sticking with something.

This story is inspired by the unparalleled journey and basketball prowess of the legendary Michael Jordan.

CHAPTER 10: EMMA'S THREE-POINT TRIUMPH

In the heart of the busy town of Splash City, where rolling hills meet sparkling streams, basketball was more than just a sport—it was a tradition. Every weekend, as the sun painted the sky with shades of gold and red, kids would talk excitedly and playfully challenge each other on the local basketball court. The rhythmic bounce of basketballs and the echo of laughter filled the air, making a charming symphony of hopes and dreams.

There were a lot of young kids who wanted to play hoops, but one player named Emma stood out. She was hard to miss because she was tall and had a strong will. Every time she stepped onto the old court, her eyes would light up because she had one goal in mind: to learn the hard-to-get three-point shot. While the other players practiced layups and dribbling moves, Emma would stand beyond the line and work on her stance, figure out the angle, and shoot the ball with complete focus while the others were practicing layups and dribbling.

Emma wore her signature golden basketball shoes to finish off her look. They weren't just any shoes; they were her good charm, a sign of how hard she worked, and a small nod to Stephen Curry, the basketball player she looked up to. Every time she jumped, swished, or shot a three-pointer, she pictured herself playing with Curry, drawing power and inspiration from his amazing skills and love for the game.

Mockery and Motivation

In Splash City, where everyone knows each other, news spreads quickly. Many people praised Emma's determination and constant focus, but there were a few who thought she was crazy. Especially the bigger kids found it funny how hard Emma worked to perfect just one part of the game. "Why not practice a layup or a free throw?" they'd sneer, trying to make her feel less confident. "Not everyone has the magic touch for those three-pointers," they'd whisper to each other loudly enough for her to hear.

But Emma had a secret weapon: a strong spirit that never gave up. She didn't let the mean things people said about her bring her down. Instead, she turned them into fuel for her fire. Every word and smirk made her want to work even harder on her skills. She thought back to the stories about her hero, Stephen Curry, and how he had his share of doubters in the beginning of his career. How he didn't look like a typical basketball player and how his revolutionary shooting skills shut up his doubters. "He changed the game," she would say to herself as she set up for another shot, "and I can too."

Even though the lights on the court were dim, Emma's figure could be seen taking shot after shot as the crickets chirped in the background. She didn't just want to make three-pointers, she wanted to master them and make them an essential part of her game. "Every legend starts with a dream, and every critic can be shown wrong," she believed in her heart.

The Magical Mentor

Emma was in the middle of her routine, making three-pointers one after the other as the sun cast long shadows over the Splash City court. She didn't know it, but she had caught the eye of someone who was just watching. The figure was a tall, confident woman who walked slowly toward the court. She never took her eyes off of Emma.

This was Ms. Riley, a name that was revered in Splash City's basketball circles. She used to be a basketball star and was known for how well she shot, especially from beyond the hoop. Even though she hadn't played in years, she still loved the game as much as ever. She saw something in Emma that reminded her of herself. The hard work and constant attention were all too familiar.

"Your form is good, but it can be better," Ms. Riley said to break the silence. Emma listened carefully, a little surprised but still interested. Over the next few weeks, Emma learned more about shooting under the watchful eye of her new teacher. Ms. Riley gave advice on both the physical and mental parts of the game, like how to make the perfect circle and wrist flick. She stressed how important it was to stay calm under pressure and have faith in oneself, even when the risks were high. Together, they made a bond that went beyond basketball, a bond of shared dreams and unbreakable drive.

The Splash City Showdown

The sun was low in the sky, giving the Splash City Basketball Court a golden color. Everyone was there, and the air was thick with excitement. The Splash City Basketball

Championship was the best event of the year, and this year, the battle was tougher than ever. Emma's team, the Splash Sisters, had worked hard to get to the finals, where they had their sights set on the prized award. Their tough opponents, the Raging Rivers, were known for their offensive style of play and had a good record. As soon as the whistle blew to start the game, you could feel the tension.

The sounds of squeaking shoes, gasps and cheers from the crowd, and the rhythmic moving of the ball filled the court. Both teams played with great skill, and each basket was met with cheers or sighs of disappointment, based on who you were rooting for. It was a close game, and the person in the lead changed all the time. By the end of the third quarter, the Raging Rivers had made a small lead of two points. Every step was important, and every second mattered. And then, as time was running out, fate picked its moment.

The Raging Rivers missed their shot, and the ball hit the ground and landed in Emma's hands. She ran as fast as she could and got herself just outside the three-point line. The weight of the moment pushed down on her, but she thought back to all the hours of practice, Ms. Riley's helpful lessons, and Stephen Curry's amazing plays. Emma took a deep breath and then aimed and shot. The ball flew through the stress, and its path seemed to be perfect. As it fell smoothly through the hoop, everyone cheered. The three-pointer by Emma not only showed how good she was, but it also won the game for the Splash Sisters. Victory was sweet, and the trip that led to it made it even better.

The Legend of Splash City

Splash City had seen its fair share of basketball legends, but Emma's three-pointer in the title game made a stir like nothing else. Word quickly spread outside of the town, bringing fans and interested people from all over. Parents told their kids about the "Queen of the Three-Pointers," and soon there were lots of kids on basketball courts trying to copy Emma's signature shot. Every game she played was now a show, with groups gathering a long time before the game to see the new local hero in action.

Not only did Emma's amazing skills win people over, but also her hard work and never-say-die attitude. Young players now had a new role model—someone who had faced problems and been made fun of for wanting to be successful, but who had risen above it all and become successful. Splash City's basketball schools had a lot more people sign up, especially girls who thought they could be like Emma and rule the floor. "Did you see that?" rang out from playgrounds. Every time a child made a basket, they would say, "Just like Emma!"

But Emma didn't care about her fame. Her love for the game never changed in any way. She liked the attention and was happy to be an inspiration, but she kept training as hard as ever. Every day, she'd put on her shoes, think about what Ms. Riley had taught her, and get ideas from Stephen Curry's moves. Emma's journey changed basketball in Splash City and made her known as someone who not only chased success but also got it.

This story is inspired by the real-life basketball prowess and journey of Stephen Curry.

CHAPTER 11: CHRIS'S COURT VISION

In the busy center of Midtown, the tall skyscrapers made long shadows that reached down to the basketball courts. The streets were filled with the sounds of moving balls and sneaker squeaks, but one player seemed to move to a beat all his own. Chris had made a name for himself in the area with his quick moves and smart plays. People would gather and talk about that one kid who seemed to have a "magic touch" with the ball.

Chris liked basketball for more than just making good shots and hearing the net swish. It was a beautiful combination of plays, moves, and teamwork. He had an uncanny ability to see plays before they happened, making sure that his teammates were always in the spotlight. His willingness to help others and his natural ability to pass the ball around made every player around him look better, work harder, and believe more in the team's power.

Chris's style of play was very similar to that of the great Magic Johnson. Johnson changed the game with his court vision and willingness to play for the team. Midtown's prodigy seemed to be a spiritual replacement to Johnson. Chris, like Magic, wasn't just playing the game—he was running it. He turned basketball into an art form and helped everyone around him get better.

Whispers and Wonders
==

In basketball-crazy Midtown, where many kids wore jerseys of the current scoring champions, Chris's pick of hero made some people look at him funny. Chris was happy to wear the jersey of a great player from the past, Magic Johnson, instead of the flashy shooters of today. Peers would often gather around him because they were amazed by his high-flying dunks and buzzer-beater shots. "Out of all the players, why Magic Johnson?" they'd ask, really wanting to know why he had made such an unusual pick.

Chris's answer was never a long lesson on the history of basketball or a list of Magic's many accomplishments. Instead, he would smile confidently and wave his hand to get their attention. "Watch this," he'd say with a hint of mischief in his voice. Then, when everyone on the field was looking at him, Chris would pull off a beautiful no-look pass or a quick behind-the-back dribble. Each move was perfectly timed to help a teammate get an open shot. The ball would easily go into the net, and people watching would cheer and applaud in unison.

Chris's play was magical (no pun meant) not just because he was good at it, but also because of what he was trying to do. While others tried to be the center of attention, Chris loved setting up his friends and showing how well he knew the game. Anyone who watched could see that Chris wasn't just another player. He had the rare ability to look at basketball in a unique, almost poetic way, just like his hero, Magic Johnson.

Challenges and Triumphs

No matter how skilled a player is, they all face problems along the way, and Chris was no different. In the high-stakes world of Midtown hoops, Chris's skill at setting up plays was quickly noticed by other teams. As word of his skills spread, he was often suddenly surrounded by players whose goal was to stop him from moving and making decisions. The double teams against him became a common way to try to corner Chris and stop him from having an effect on the game.

But Chris didn't just like Magic Johnson because he was a great playmaker. He also liked him because he never gave up. Every time he felt pressure, Chris would think back to all the games where Magic faced impossible odds but won because he was smart and worked hard. Chris changed because of these memories. He started using fake moves to draw players to him so he could pass the ball to a teammate who wasn't being watched. As he learned more about the game, he was able to predict how the defense would play and act accordingly.

Chris's favorite places to play were the tight spots that most people saw as pressure points. When time was running out and the game was still close, Chris's teammates always knew they could trust what he saw. His ability to think several moves ahead made him more than just a good player; it made him Midtown's best strategist. Chris's smart approach to the game often turned out to be the secret tool that tipped the scales in Midtown's favor during those close games.

The Midtown Magic Moment

It was very exciting to be in Midtown. There was only one thing people talked about everywhere, from street corners to cafes: the citywide basketball tourney. Chris, the playmaking genius who had taken the local basketball scene by storm, led the Midtown Mavericks to the finals. Fans of all ages were excitedly waiting for the matchup, and you could feel the tension in the air. But it wasn't going to be easy to get to the title. Their opponents were a strong team known for their tough defense, quick interceptions, and amazing ability to block even the hardest shots.

At the start of the final game, both teams were in a fierce fight, trying to figure out how to beat the other. The other team seemed to have done their study because there were always defenders around Chris, waiting for him to move. As the game went on, it was clear that each point would be hard-fought. With the scores tied and just seconds left on the clock, Midtown's hopes were all on the Mavericks. Chris got the ball and dribbled his way through the court to get it. As players closed in on him, everyone knew he would take the shot that could have won the game.

But Chris was thinking of something else. Using his huge bag of tricks and natural feel for the game, he cleverly got several players to come to him, which took their attention away from the real threat. Just as everyone was getting ready to take a shot, Chris, with perfect timing, made a perfect pass to a friend who was unmarked. The ball went right through the net without stopping. When the buzzer went off, everyone in the room cheered. The Midtown Mavericks had won the championship against all odds. As Chris's teammates lifted him up in celebration, there was no question in anyone's mind: Chris had not only led his team to victory, but he had also made his name even more famous in Midtown, drawing comparisons to the great "Magic" Johnson himself.

This story is inspired by the legendary basketball prowess and playmaking abilities of Magic Johnson.

CHAPTER 12: BASKETBALL'S HEARTWARMING MOMENTS

Basketballs and Bookbags

In the small town of Riverdale, the local school's basketball court was more than just a place to play. Every summer, the Riverdale Rockets basketball team organized a charity event where kids could trade in their gently used books for a chance to play basketball with the team. Not only did this promote reading, but it also allowed children from different backgrounds to bond over the love of the game. The donated books were then given to local libraries and children in need. Basketball became a bridge to knowledge and friendship in Riverdale.

The Reunion Game

Years ago, in the vibrant city of Sunnyside, two rival basketball teams, the Sunnyside Stars and the Moonlight Mavericks, always competed fiercely. Their rivalry was known throughout the city. But as time passed and players grew older, the rivalry faded. Decades later, the teams decided to have a reunion game, not as competitors but as friends celebrating their shared history. The entire city gathered, old tales were retold, and everyone celebrated the unity that the sport brought them. The match ended in a tie, symbolizing their newfound camaraderie.

One Shot at Hope

In a bustling urban center known as Metroville, a young girl named Lily, who was battling a serious illness, had a dream: to shoot a basket on her favorite team's home court. When the Metroville Titans heard about this, they invited Lily to a game. During halftime, with thousands of fans cheering her on, Lily took her shot and made it. The joy in her eyes and the roaring applause was a testament to how basketball could light up even the darkest moments.

The Unity Tournament

After a major storm hit the coastal town of Seaview, many of its community centers, including the beloved basketball court, were damaged. To raise funds for the repairs, neighboring towns came together to host a "Unity Tournament." Teams from all around participated, showing that basketball was more than just a game—it was a way to bring communities together. The Seaview court was rebuilt, but the unity the tournament fostered lived on, creating annual Unity Tournaments to strengthen community ties.

A Slam Dunk Birthday

Timmy, a young boy from the town of Greenfield, was a huge basketball fan but had never had the chance to see a live game. On his tenth birthday, his classmates surprised him with tickets to see his favorite team, the Greenfield

Giants, play. The look of pure joy on Timmy's face as he entered the stadium, the crowd singing 'Happy Birthday,' and his favorite player giving him a signed basketball showed just how magical and transformative the sport could be.

These heartwarming moments remind us that basketball is more than just a sport; it's a catalyst for creating bonds, memories, and positive changes in countless lives.

Conclusion: Dream, Believe, Achieve

The power of basketball stretches far beyond the confines of a court. It's more than just a game of hoops, dribbles, and slam dunks. At its core, basketball teaches us about life's most valuable lessons. And for our young readers, it's a beacon of hope, determination, and resilience.

Dreaming Big

Every young player starts with a dream. Whether it's making the school team, scoring the winning basket, or simply mastering a new trick, these dreams are the seeds of greatness. Just like Emma from Splash City, who dared to perfect her three-point shot, or Chris from Midtown, whose court vision was second to none. Their stories remind us that our dreams are valid. They teach our young readers to dream without boundaries and to see possibilities where others see challenges.

The Power of Belief

It's one thing to dream, but another to believe in that dream. The journey isn't always smooth; there will be hurdles, naysayers, and moments of doubt. But it's the unwavering belief in oneself that propels us forward. Think about the times Emma faced mockery, or when Chris was double-teamed, trying to break his rhythm. They had every reason to give up, but they didn't. Their belief in their abilities, fueled by their passion and love for the game, kept them going. And it's this same belief that our young readers must cultivate. When they believe in themselves, the impossible becomes possible.

Achieving Greatness

Achievement isn't just about winning or being the best. It's also about growing, learning, and leaving a mark. Basketball teaches players how to work as a team, follow rules, and keep going even when things get tough. When the Riverdale Rockets gave books in return for basketball, they showed how important it is to help others. When the Sunnyside Stars and Moonlight Mavericks got back together, they showed how strong friendship and unity can be. These and many other stories show young people that the road to greatness is full of ups and downs. It's about getting back up when you fall, being happy about the small wins, and always trying to do better.

Every move, pass, and shot in basketball can teach you something. For our young readers, these stories are more than just court stories; they are also lessons about life. Lessons that make them want to think big, have faith in themselves, and do their best. As a basketball flies toward the basket, may our readers also aim high and make every shot count with determination and heart.

BONUS 1: POSITIVE AFFIRMATIONS FOR SUCCESS

1. I am unique and special in my own way.
2. I love and accept myself just as I am.
3. I believe in my abilities and talents.
4. I am capable of achieving great things.
5. I am full of endless possibilities.
6. I am confident in everything I do.
7. I am kind and compassionate towards others.
8. I choose to focus on the positive in every situation.
9. I am a source of positivity and light.
10. I am resilient and can overcome any challenge.
11. I am loved and cherished by my family and friends.
12. I have a bright and happy future ahead of me.
13. I am a good friend to others.
14. I am grateful for the little things in life.
15. I am a lifelong learner, and I love to learn new things.
16. I am in control of my thoughts and feelings.
17. I am always learning and growing.
18. I am surrounded by love and support.
19. I am open to new experiences and adventures.
20. I am a positive role model for others.
21. I am full of energy and enthusiasm.
22. I am capable of making a positive impact on the world.
23. I am responsible and make good choices.
24. I am confident in expressing my ideas and opinions.
25. I am a problem solver and can find solutions.
26. I am worthy of love and respect.
27. I am a good listener and a caring friend.
28. I am always improving and getting better.
29. I am patient and understanding.
30. I am brave and can face my fears.
31. I am a source of joy and laughter.
32. I am proud of my accomplishments, big or small.

33. I am loved for who I am, not just what I do.
34. I am a creative thinker and can find unique solutions.
35. I am honest and true to myself.
36. I am capable of achieving my dreams.
37. I am kind to myself, especially when things are tough.
38. I am in charge of my own happiness.
39. I am a positive influence on those around me.
40. I am a good team player and work well with others.
41. I am always learning from my mistakes.
42. I am strong and can handle whatever comes my way.
43. I am surrounded by beauty and wonder in the world.
44. I am a source of inspiration for others.
45. I am a leader and can lead by example.
46. I am grateful for the love and support in my life.
47. I am open to new friendships and connections.
48. I am a good problem solver and can find solutions.
49. I am resilient and can bounce back from setbacks.
50. I am capable of achieving my goals.
51. I am a positive force in the world.
52. I am always learning and growing.
53. I am patient with myself and others.
54. I am capable of handling change and uncertainty.
55. I am a good decision-maker.
56. I am loved unconditionally.
57. I am a source of positivity and light.
58. I am kind and compassionate.
59. I am capable of making a difference in the world.
60. I am confident in my abilities.
61. I am full of creativity and imagination.
62. I am a good friend to others.
63. I am in control of my thoughts and feelings.
64. I am grateful for the love in my life.
65. I am a lifelong learner.
66. I am capable of achieving my dreams.
67. I am loved and cherished.
68. I am a source of joy and happiness.
69. I am responsible and make good choices.

70. I am confident in expressing myself.
71. I am always improving and growing.
72. I am patient and understanding.
73. I am brave and can face challenges head-on.
74. I am proud of my accomplishments.
75. I am capable of overcoming obstacles.
76. I am worthy of love and respect.
77. I am a good listener and friend.
78. I am always learning from my experiences.
79. I am strong and resilient.
80. I am surrounded by beauty and goodness.
81. I am a positive role model for others.
82. I am a leader and can inspire others.
83. I am open to new opportunities.
84. I am a problem solver and can find solutions.
85. I am honest and true to myself.
86. I am capable of achieving my goals.
87. I am kind to myself and others.
88. I am in charge of my own happiness.
89. I am a good team player and collaborator.
90. I am capable of handling challenges.
91. I am a source of inspiration for others.
92. I am always learning and growing.
93. I am patient and compassionate.
94. I am confident in my abilities.
95. I am a positive force in the world.
96. I am responsible and make good choices.
97. I am resilient and can bounce back from setbacks.
98. I am capable of achieving my dreams.
99. I am filled with love, happiness, and self-esteem.
100. I am a source of kindness and positivity.
101. I am a beacon of hope for those around me.
102. I am capable of handling whatever comes my way.
103. I am a loving and caring person.
104. I am always open to new possibilities.
105. I am filled with gratitude for the present moment.
106. I am a source of inspiration to others.

107. I am a responsible and dependable friend.
108. I am confident in my ability to learn and grow.
109. I am surrounded by opportunities for success.
110. I am a good problem solver and can find answers.
111. I am resilient and can adapt to change.
112. I am a positive influence on my peers.
113. I am a magnet for good things to come my way.
114. I am full of creativity and innovative ideas.
115. I am proud of the person I am becoming.
116. I am a loving and supportive family member.
117. I am always seeking ways to improve myself.
118. I am confident in expressing my true self.
119. I am capable of turning challenges into opportunities.
120. I am a source of joy and laughter for others.
121. I am grateful for the lessons I learn every day.
122. I am a compassionate and empathetic listener.
123. I am courageous and stand up for what is right.
124. I am a source of positivity in my community.
125. I am full of energy and enthusiasm for life.
126. I am capable of achieving my wildest dreams.
127. I am responsible for my own happiness.
128. I am a good communicator and can express myself well.
129. I am always open to learning from others.
130. I am strong and resilient, like a tree in a storm.
131. I am a friend who can be trusted and relied upon.
132. I am open to new experiences that expand my horizons.
133. I am a beacon of light even in the darkest moments.
134. I am surrounded by love and support every day.
135. I am a positive force for change in the world.
136. I am full of curiosity and a thirst for knowledge.
137. I am a good sport and can handle wins and losses gracefully.
138. I am confident in my ability to make a difference.
139. I am patient with myself and others.
140. I am capable of finding solutions to any problem.
141. I am worthy of all the good things that come my way.
142. I am a friend who brings joy to others.

143. I am in control of my own destiny.
144. I am open to new friendships and connections.
145. I am capable of achieving my highest goals.
146. I am a positive role model for those younger than me.
147. I am a loving and giving person.
148. I am always striving to be the best version of myself.
149. I am confident in my ability to handle adversity.
150. I am a source of happiness to my loved ones.
151. I am grateful for the simple pleasures in life.
152. I am a source of encouragement to others.
153. I am a responsible and reliable member of my family.
154. I am open to the wisdom of those who came before me.
155. I am strong and unshakable in my beliefs.
156. I am a good leader and inspire others to follow.
157. I am capable of achieving my dreams through hard work.
158. I am kind to myself, especially during difficult times.
159. I am a positive influence on my peers.
160. I am a magnet for success and happiness.
161. I am a creative problem solver.
162. I am proud of my accomplishments and achievements.
163. I am a source of comfort and support to others.
164. I am always open to new adventures.
165. I am surrounded by love and positive energy.
166. I am a force for good in the world.
167. I am curious and eager to explore new ideas.
168. I am a good sport and show sportsmanship in all I do.
169. I am confident in my ability to make a positive impact.
170. I am patient with myself as I grow and learn.
171. I am capable of finding solutions to challenges.
172. I am worthy of all the love and happiness in the world.
173. I am a friend who brings joy and laughter to others.
174. I am in charge of my own destiny and choices.
175. I am open to new friendships and connections.
176. I am capable of reaching my highest aspirations.
177. I am a positive example for my peers.
178. I am a source of love and kindness.
179. I am always striving to improve and learn.

180. I am confident in my ability to overcome obstacles.
181. I am a source of inspiration and motivation.
182. I am grateful for the love and support in my life.
183. I am responsible and make choices that align with my values.
184. I am resilient and can bounce back from challenges.
185. I am capable of achieving my dreams through hard work.
186. I am filled with love, kindness, and positivity.
187. I am open to new experiences that enrich my life.
188. I am a positive force for change in my community.
189. I am a continuous learner, always seeking knowledge.
190. I am confident in my abilities and talents.
191. I am a gracious winner and a good loser.
192. I am proud of my accomplishments, no matter how big or small.
193. I am a source of encouragement to my loved ones.
194. I am always open to new opportunities.
195. I am surrounded by love and positive energy every day.
196. I am a beacon of light even in challenging times.
197. I am confident in my ability to handle whatever comes my way.
198. I am a loving and caring friend to others.
199. I am full of gratitude for the present moment.
200. Keep these affirmations in mind and repeat them regularly to boost your self-esteem and bring more happiness into your life!
201. I am a unique and valuable person.
202. I radiate positivity wherever I go.
203. I believe in my dreams and work toward them.
204. I am a source of love and compassion.
205. I am a magnet for success and happiness.
206. I trust in my ability to handle challenges.
207. I am a source of inspiration to my peers.
208. I am open to the beauty of the world around me.
209. I am resilient and bounce back from setbacks.
210. I am a force for good in my community.
211. I embrace change as an opportunity for growth.

212. I am a caring and empathetic listener.
213. I am confident in my decision-making skills.
214. I am grateful for the abundance in my life.
215. I am a kind and considerate friend.
216. I am a lifelong learner and embrace new knowledge.
217. I am in control of my thoughts and emotions.
218. I am a leader who leads with kindness.
219. I am open to the endless possibilities of life.
220. I am a creative problem solver.
221. I am proud of my achievements, no matter the size.
222. I am a source of encouragement to those in need.
223. I am always ready for exciting adventures.
224. I am surrounded by love and positive vibes.
225. I am a catalyst for positive change in the world.
226. I am curious and eager to explore the world.
227. I am a gracious winner and a good loser.
228. I am confident in my ability to make a difference.
229. I am patient with myself as I grow and learn.
230. I am capable of finding solutions to any challenge.
231. I am worthy of all the good things in life.
232. I am a friend who brings happiness to others.
233. I am the captain of my own destiny.
234. I am open to forming meaningful friendships.
235. I am capable of reaching for the stars.
236. I am a positive role model for my peers.
237. I am a source of love and kindness.
238. I am always striving for self-improvement.
239. I am confident in my ability to overcome adversity.
240. I am grateful for the love and support in my life.
241. I am responsible and make choices that align with my values.
242. I am resilient and can bounce back from challenges.
243. I am capable of achieving my dreams through hard work.
244. I am filled with love, kindness, and positivity.
245. I am open to new experiences that enrich my life.
246. I am a positive force for change in my community.
247. I am a continuous learner, always seeking knowledge.

248. I am confident in my abilities and talents.
249. I am a gracious winner and a good loser.
250. I am proud of my accomplishments, no matter how big or small.
251. I am a source of encouragement to my loved ones.
252. I am always open to new opportunities.
253. I am surrounded by love and positive energy every day.
254. I am a beacon of light even in challenging times.
255. I am confident in my ability to handle whatever comes my way.
256. I am a loving and caring friend to others.
257. I am full of gratitude for the present moment.
258. I am a source of joy and happiness.
259. I am a positive influence on my peers.
260. I am a magnet for success and prosperity.
261. I am a creative problem solver.
262. I am proud of my accomplishments and achievements.
263. I am a source of encouragement to my loved ones.
264. I am always open to new opportunities.
265. I am surrounded by love and positive energy every day.
266. I am a beacon of light even in challenging times.
267. I am confident in my ability to handle whatever comes my way.
268. I am a loving and caring friend to others.
269. I am full of gratitude for the present moment.
270. I am a source of joy and happiness.
271. I am a positive influence on my peers.
272. I am a magnet for success and prosperity.
273. I am confident in my ability to achieve my goals.
274. I am open to receiving love and support from others.
275. I am responsible for my own happiness.
276. I am a source of motivation to those around me.
277. I am resilient and can overcome any obstacle.
278. I am capable of accomplishing great things.
279. I am a beacon of positivity in the world.
280. I am a source of comfort to my loved ones.
281. I am always open to new experiences.

282. I am surrounded by abundance and prosperity.
283. I am a catalyst for positive change in my community.
284. I am a constant learner and love acquiring knowledge.
285. I am confident in my unique talents and gifts.
286. I am open to new challenges that help me grow.
287. I am a source of encouragement to those in need.
288. I am capable of making a lasting impact on the world.
289. I am full of optimism and hope for the future.
290. I am a positive force in the lives of others.
291. I am grateful for the lessons I learn from every experience.
292. I am a reliable and trustworthy friend.
293. I am open to the wisdom of those who came before me.
294. I am strong and unwavering in my beliefs.
295. I am a leader who guides with compassion.
296. I am capable of turning my dreams into reality.
297. I am kind to myself, especially in challenging moments.
298. I am a beacon of inspiration to those around me.
299. I am filled with self-love, happiness, and confidence.

BONUS 2: BASKETBALL KNOWLEDGE QUIZ FOR TEENS

Welcome to the Basketball Knowledge Quiz for Teens!

Test your basketball IQ by answering these questions. Choose the best answer for each question, and then check your answers at the end to see how much you know about the sport. Good luck!

PART 1

1. How many players are on the court for each team in a standard basketball game?
a) 4
b) 5
c) 6
d) 7

2. Who is often referred to as "The Greek Freak" and plays for the Milwaukee Bucks?
a) LeBron James
b) Stephen Curry
c) Giannis Antetokounmpo
d) Kevin Durant

3. What is the name of the hoop in basketball that is made of a metal ring and a net?

a) Goalpost

b) Rim

c) Loop

d) Ringlet

4. Which NBA team has won the most championships in league history?

a) Boston Celtics

b) Los Angeles Lakers

c) Chicago Bulls

d) Golden State Warriors

5. What is the term for a shot that is worth three points because it's taken from beyond the three-point line?

a) Free throw

b) Slam dunk

c) Three-pointer

d) Layup

6. Who is often credited with inventing the game of basketball in 1891?

a) Michael Jordan

b) Kobe Bryant

c) Dr. James Naismith

d) Larry Bird

7. Which two colleges have a legendary basketball rivalry known as the "Duke vs. North Carolina" rivalry?

a) Georgetown vs. Syracuse
b) Kansas vs. Kentucky
c) UCLA vs. Arizona
d) Duke vs. North Carolina

8. Who holds the record for the most points scored in a single NBA game with 100 points?
a) LeBron James
b) Kobe Bryant
c) Michael Jordan
d) Wilt Chamberlain

9. Which position on a basketball team is typically responsible for playmaking and assists?
a) Center
b) Shooting guard
c) Point guard
d) Power forward

10. Which NBA legend is known for his famous "Sky Hook" shot and played for the Los Angeles Lakers?
a) Magic Johnson
b) Larry Bird
c) Shaquille O'Neal
d) Kareem Abdul-Jabbar

Answers:

b) 5
c) Giannis Antetokounmpo
b) Rim
b) Los Angeles Lakers
c) Three-pointer
c) Dr. James Naismith
d) Duke vs. North Carolina
d) Wilt Chamberlain
c) Point guard
d) Kareem Abdul-Jabbar

PART 2

1. What is the name of the NBA team based in Miami, Florida?
a) Chicago Bulls
b) Boston Celtics
c) Los Angeles Lakers
d) Miami Heat

2. Which award is given to the NBA player who demonstrates the best sportsmanship and ethical behavior on and off the court?
a) MVP Award
b) Rookie of the Year
c) Sixth Man of the Year
d) NBA Cares Community Assist Award

3. How long is the three-point line in NBA basketball?
a) 15 feet
b) 20 feet
c) 23.75 feet
d) 25 feet

4. Who holds the record for the most career points scored in NBA history?
a) Michael Jordan
b) Kobe Bryant
c) LeBron James

d) Kareem Abdul-Jabbar

5. What term is used to describe a defensive play where a player jumps and tries to block or deflect a shot without making physical contact with the shooter?
a) Foul
b) Rebound
c) Steal
d) Block

6. In which year did basketball become an official Olympic sport?
a) 1900
b) 1932
c) 1960
d) 1984

7. Who is known as the "Zen Master" and coached the Chicago Bulls and the Los Angeles Lakers to multiple NBA championships?
a) Gregg Popovich
b) Pat Riley
c) Phil Jackson
d) Red Auerbach

8. What is the highest number of points scored by a single player in an NBA game, excluding Wilt Chamberlain's famous 100-point game?
a) 81

b) 73
c) 70
d) 65

9. Which NBA player is known for his nickname "The Answer" and played primarily for the Philadelphia 76ers?
a) Allen Iverson
b) Tracy McGrady
c) Dwyane Wade
d) Vince Carter

20. What is the regulation height of an NBA basketball hoop from the floor?
a) 8 feet
b) 9 feet
c) 10 feet
d) 12 feet

Answers:
d) Miami Heat
d) NBA Cares Community Assist Award
c) 23.75 feet
d) Kareem Abdul-Jabbar
d) Block
b) 1932
c) Phil Jackson
a) 81

a) Allen Iverson

c) 10 feet

PART 3

1. Which college basketball team is known for its historic and dominating run during the 1960s, winning seven consecutive NCAA championships from 1967 to 1973?

a) Kentucky Wildcats

b) North Carolina Tar Heels

c) UCLA Bruins

d) Duke Blue Devils

2. Who holds the record for the most assists in a single NBA game with 30 assists?

a) Chris Paul

b) Steve Nash

c) John Stockton

d) Magic Johnson

3. What term is used to describe a player's ability to dribble past defenders while maintaining control of the ball, often displayed by skilled point guards?

a) Slam dunk

b) Crossover

c) Fast break

d) Pick and roll

4. Which NBA player is known for his iconic skywalking dunks and played for the Chicago Bulls during the 1980s and 1990s?
a) Larry Bird
b) Hakeem Olajuwon
c) Shaquille O'Neal
d) Michael Jordan

5. Which country's men's basketball team is known as the "Dream Team" for their outstanding performance in the 1992 Summer Olympics?
a) United States
b) Spain
c) Russia
d) France

6. How long is the shot clock in NBA basketball, giving teams a limited amount of time to attempt a shot?
a) 24 seconds
b) 30 seconds
c) 35 seconds
d) 40 seconds

7. Who is often called the "Black Mamba" and is considered one of the greatest shooting guards in NBA history?
a) Tim Duncan
b) Karl Malone

c) Kevin Garnett

d) Kobe Bryant

8. **What is the name of the annual college basketball tournament that features 68 college teams competing for the national championship?**

a) College Slam

b) March Madness

c) Elite Eight

d) Final Four

9. **Which player holds the record for the most triple-doubles in NBA history?**

a) Russell Westbrook

b) LeBron James

c) Oscar Robertson

d) Magic Johnson

10. **Which basketball movie features the fictional team the "Monstars" who steal the basketball skills of NBA players?**

a) Space Jam

b) Hoosiers

c) Coach Carter

d) White Men Can't Jump

Answers:

c) UCLA Bruins

d) Magic Johnson

b) Crossover

d) Michael Jordan

a) United States

a) 24 seconds

d) Kobe Bryant

b) March Madness

c) Oscar Robertson

a) Space Jam

Calculate your score out of 30 based on your correct answers from all three sets of questions to determine your basketball knowledge level.

0-9 correct answers: You're just getting started! Keep learning about basketball.

10-18 correct answers: Nice job! You know some basketball basics.

19-25 correct answers: Impressive! You're a true basketball enthusiast.

26-30 correct answers: Slam dunk! You're a basketball expert!

Do Not Go Yet; One Last Thing To Do

If you enjoyed this book or found it useful, I'd be very grateful if you'd post a short review on Amazon. Your support does make a difference, and I read all the reviews personally so I can get your feedback and make this book even better.

Thanks again for your support!

Made in the USA
Middletown, DE
17 December 2023